D1298841

THAT'S ENTERTAINING!
COCKTAILS AND APPETIZERS

WITH TIM LAIRD, AMERICA'S C.E.O. *CHIEF ENTERTAINING OFFICER*

THAT'S ENTERTAINING!

COCKTAILS AND APPETIZERS

WITH TIM LAIRD, AMERICA'S C.E.O. *CHIEF ENTERTAINING OFFICER*

PHOTOGRAPHY BY DAN DRY

Butler Books

ISBN 978-1-935497-74-5

Printed in Canada

Photography © 2013 by Dan Dry

Many of the products featured in the recipes in *That's Entertaining! Cocktails and Appetizers* are registered trademarks. The authors would like to acknowledge the owners of those products in the following list:

Jack Daniel's, Jack Daniel's Tennessee Honey and any of the Jack Daniel's family of brands are registered trademarks of Jack Daniel's.

Canadian Mist, Chambord, el Jimador, Herradura and Woodford Reserve are registered trademarks of Brown-Forman Corporation.

Southern Comfort is a registered trademark of Southern Comfort.

Early Times and Old Forester are registered trademarks of Early Times Distillers Company.

Sonoma-Cutter is a registered trademark of Sonoma-Cutter Vineyards.

Finlandia is a registered trademark of Finlandia Vodka Worldwide.

Korbel is a registered trademark.

Little Black Dress is a registered trademark.

Tuaca is a registered trademark.

Angostura Bitters is a registered trademark.

Finest Call is a registered trademark of American Beverage Marketers.

Luxardo is a registered trademark.

Sprite, Fresca and Dasani are registered trademarks of Coca-Cola Company.

Rice Krispies is a registered trademark of Kellogg NA Co.

Ocean Spray is a registered trademark of Ocean Spray Cranberries, Inc.

Noilly Pratt is a registered trademark of Ets. Noilly Prat & Cie.

Campari is a registered trademark of Gruppo Campari.

Goslings Rum is a registered trademark of Gosling Brothers.

Fee Brothers Bitters is a registered trademark of Fee Brothers.

Book design by Scott Stortz

Butler Books
P.O. Box 7311
Louisville, KY 40257
Phone (502) 897-9393
Fax (502) 897-9797

www.butlerbooks.com

We would like to thank our friends and family and especially those who shared their favorite recipes with us.

A big "Cheers!" goes out to our designer, photographer and publisher.

We truly appreciate our friends at Brown-Forman for keeping the party going.

CONTENTS

INTRODUCTION

The new trend in entertaining at home is that everything, including cocktails and appetizers, should be easy to make and easy to serve. A host's focus should be on getting together with friends and family for fun, without a lot of stress.

To help you plan a party that is both stress-free and successful, I have compiled a variety of cocktail and appetizer ideas that should ease the process for you.

Each chapter is divided into spirit categories, and I have included a chapter with lower-calorie mixers (Skinny Cocktails) and alcohol-free cocktails (Mocktails). Also woven in is a little history and lore on each spirit, along with interesting stories on some of the cocktails. At the end of the book you will find a list of basic bar tools and glassware, cocktail tips and checklists, quantities needed for parties, and syrup recipes that are helpful.

Always remember to be a responsible host and offer your guests plenty of food and alcohol-free beverages.

I hope this book provides you with ideas and inspiration as you choose the perfect cocktails and appetizers for your next party.

Cheers!

BOURBON

Bourbon has an amazing American heritage and is becoming more popular and high in demand, globally. An interesting fact is: all bourbons are whiskeys but not all whiskeys are bourbons. To be called bourbon, it must follow these strict guidelines:

1. It must contain, in its mash bill (makeup of grains cooked in water with a combination of corn, wheat, rye and/or barley), at least 51% corn.
2. It must be aged in new, charred oak barrels.
3. It must be bottled at a minimum of 80 proof or 40% alcohol by volume.
4. It must be made in America. Interestingly, most bourbon comes from Kentucky. Why Kentucky? Many distillers found a great water source there which contained a lot of limestone and minerals. The distillers discovered this water made the best bourbon. Also, there was an abundance of corn, the primary ingredient in bourbon. Another hallmark of Kentucky is its cold winters and hot summers. This change in temperature allows the bourbon to breathe in and out of the charred oak barrel which gives the bourbon its color and many of its flavor and taste characteristics.

Other than in cocktails, a great way to enjoy bourbon is poured over one ice cube in a rocks glass. If you are at Churchill Downs on the first Saturday in May, you most likely will be drinking your bourbon in a Mint Julep.

Cheers!

MANHATTAN

This drink exemplifies the true definition of a cocktail which is a combination of: a spirit, sugar, water and bitters. The sweet flavor comes from an Italian sweet vermouth. For an even sweeter style, some add a little cherry juice. The cocktail was supposedly invented in Manhattan, New York. Many debates of where and how still ensue.

In a mixing glass with ice, add:
2 ounces Woodford Reserve bourbon
¾ ounce sweet vermouth
3 dashes Angostura bitters

Stir vigorously and strain into a chilled martini glass.
Garnish with a maraschino cherry.

Note: The Luxardo brand makes a classic cherry which is delicious.

SWEET AND SPICY NUTS

1 pound raw nuts *(pecans, walnuts, almonds, cashews or any combination)*
1 egg white
1 tablespoon water
1 cup sugar
1 teaspoon salt
1 teaspoon cinnamon
½ teaspoon cayenne pepper

Preheat oven to 200 degrees.

In a large bowl, beat the egg white and water until frothy, but not stiff. Stir in sugar, salt, cinnamon and cayenne. Add nuts and stir until completely coated. Spread nuts on a large baking sheet and bake for 45 minutes, stirring every 15 minutes. Remove from the oven when dry and toasty. When cool, store in an airtight container.

OLD FASHIONED

Many say this cocktail was invented at the Pendennis Club in Louisville, Kentucky. However, many also say this cocktail was made long before the club opened in 1881. What made it famous at the Pendennis Club is customers would order this drink by saying, "I'll have a cocktail, but make it the old-fashioned way."

The bourbon used in this cocktail was the first bottled bourbon and hails from Kentucky. This cocktail has evolved from the original bourbon, sugar, bitters and citrus to a drink with club soda or lemon-lime soda, muddled fruit and other items but this is the classic recipe:

In an old-fashioned glass, add:
1 ounce Simple Syrup (page 202) or one sugar cube
2 dashes bitters
Two-inch disk of orange peel

Gently muddle (not pulverize) to release the oils.
Add 2 ounces Old Forester bourbon
Stir, add a large ice cube and garnish with an additional orange peel.

BOURBON BEE

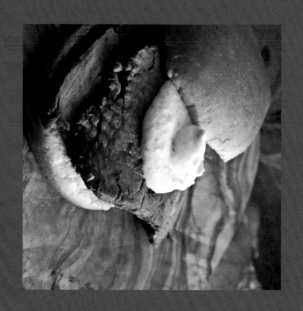

This cocktail was developed to mask the flavors of not-so-great tasting whiskeys in the 1800s. They sweetened the whiskey by adding honey syrup to improve the taste. Today, using great hand-crafted bourbon makes this cocktail one to buzz about.

In a shaker with ice, add:
2 ounces Woodford Reserve bourbon
¾ ounce Honey Syrup (page 203)
½ ounce fresh lemon juice
Shake and strain into a martini glass.
Garnish with a lemon twist.

BEEF TENDERLOIN SLIDERS

If you do not have time to cook your own beef tenderloin, pick it up already cooked from your favorite market or the prepared food area of your local grocery store and have it sliced thick (¼-inch). Place a slice or two of beef on a "slider" or mini hamburger bun and add the Horseradish Dijon Cream or serve it on the side.

HORSERADISH DIJON CREAM

In a small bowl, combine:
1 cup sour cream or non-fat plain yogurt (preferably Greek-style)
¼ cup horseradish
2 tablespoons Dijon mustard
½ teaspoon Kosher salt
½ teaspoon black pepper

BOURBON BREEZE

This is a light and refreshing bourbon cocktail which can be enjoyed in the summertime when the weather is warm. Make a pitcher by multiplying the recipe and adding water to adjust the taste.

In a shaker with ice, add:
1½ ounces bourbon
2 ounces lemonade
1 ounce pomegranate juice

Shake and strain into a tall glass with ice. Garnish with a lemon wedge.

BOURBON PEACH COOLER

Bourbon and peach make for a wonderful pair. Try bourbon with peach nectar as an alternative.

In a shaker with ice, add:

1½ ounces bourbon
½ ounce peach schnapps
1 ounce unsweetened iced tea
1 dash peach bitters (optional)

Shake vigorously and pour over ice. Garnish with a peach slice.

BOURBON AND PECAN BRIE

½ cup pure maple syrup
½ cup chopped pecans
¼ cup Woodford Reserve bourbon
1 small (9-ounce) wheel Brie, room temperature
1 baguette, sliced

Serves 6-8

Combine syrup, pecans and bourbon in a small pan and simmer over low heat for 5 minutes. Pierce the brie with a fork and pour the sauce over the top. Serve with baguette slices.

HORSES NECK

This cocktail was named for the garnish which looks as if a horse is peeking out of the top of the glass. The trick is to peel a lemon by starting from the top and running a paring knife or peeler around the lemon, working your way to the bottom.

In a tall glass, add:
Lemon peel garnish from top to bottom with some hanging over the top.

Then add:
Ice
1½ ounces bourbon
4 ounces ginger ale

MINT JULEP

The most famous place to enjoy a Mint Julep is Churchill Downs, especially during the Kentucky Derby. Surprisingly, this grand old drink of the South was first used for medicinal purposes. It was known as a "morning bracer" to help ease sore muscles from the previous day's hard work on the farm. To help the whiskey go down, sugar and mint were added.

2 ounces Woodford Reserve bourbon
1 ounce Mint Simple Syrup (page 202)
Crushed ice
Mint sprig

Fill a tall glass or julep cup with crushed ice. Add the syrup, then the bourbon. Top with more crushed ice, add a sipping straw, then garnish with a mint sprig.

To make by the pitcher:
16 ounces Woodford Reserve bourbon
8 ounces Mint Simple Syrup (page 202)
Crushed Ice
Mint sprigs

Combine the bourbon and syrup in a pitcher. Pour into tall glasses or julep cups filled with crushed ice, then garnish with mint sprigs.

Serves 8

DESSERT COCKTAILS

Cocktails have always enhanced the dining occasion. They are often the perfect aperitif to stimulate the palate. They also pair well with appetizers or entrées, act as a digestive after a meal and can be the perfect dessert. Dessert cocktails were classics in the past and are coming back in style as people are looking for a fun, liquid, sweet ending to their dining experience. Popular after-dinner cocktails, including the Grasshopper, Pink Squirrel, Brandy Alexander, and many others, were typically made with either ice cream or heavy cream, along with a spirit and/or flavored spirits. I have included a couple of classic recipes in this section, and am introducing a few new dessert cocktails to try. So, with that, dessert is poured.

Cheers!

CHOCOLATE MARTINI

In a shaker with ice, add:

1½ ounces Finlandia vodka

1 ounce white chocolate liqueur

2 ounces heavy cream

Shake and strain into a martini glass rimmed with dark chocolate. Add a dash of cocoa powder on top of the cocktail.

Note: To rim the glass, melt dark chocolate on a plate in the microwave, then dip the glass into the melted chocolate and let it set.

CHOCOLATE CUPS WITH FRUIT

These are very easy to make and they are delicious. Buy pre-made chocolate cups and fill them with mini melon balls or berries. Garnish with a mint sprig.

CHOCOLATE ICE-BOX PIE

This recipe was my favorite as a kid and has been passed down through many generations.

1 9-ounce package chocolate wafers, crushed, reserve some for garnish
6 tablespoons butter, melted (for crust) plus 8 tablespoons butter, softened
2 cups confectioners' sugar
2 ounces bittersweet chocolate, melted
1 teaspoon vanilla
½ cup chopped pecans, toasted
3 egg yolks, beaten
3 egg whites, beaten stiff
½ gallon vanilla ice cream

Preheat oven to 350 degrees.

In a bowl, combine the crushed wafers and melted butter. Pour into 11 x 7-inch pan and press down firmly to form a crust. Bake for 10 minutes. Cool completely.

In a large bowl, cream the sugar, softened butter and melted chocolate. Stir in the vanilla, nuts and egg yolks. Fold in the egg whites. Pour on top of the crust and spread evenly with a spatula. Spread ice cream or slice and place on top of the chocolate mixture. Top with remaining chocolate crumbs. Freeze.

To serve, cut into squares.

Serves 16-18

CHOCOLATE ICE-BOX PIE
(Louise Hueston's)

2 cups powdered sugar
2 squares cooking chocolate
1/2 c. butter
1/2 cup nuts (chopped)
egg yolks (beaten)
egg whites (beaten stiff)

1 teasp. vanilla
1 box vanilla wafers

Method.
Cream powdered sugar, butter and melted chocolate.
Add 1 teasp. vanilla and nuts.
yolks and fold in egg whites.
1 box vanilla wafers

RASPBERRY CHEESECAKE MARTINI

In a shaker with ice, add:

1 ounce Finlandia vodka

1 ounce Chambord liqueur

1 ounce heavy cream

½ ounce lemonade

Shake and strain into a martini glass rimmed with graham cracker crumbs.

Note: To rim the glass, run a lemon wedge around the outside edge of the glass, then dip the glass into a plate of graham cracker crumbs.

GRILLED POUND CAKE WITH BERRIES

6 ½-inch thick slices pound cake

6 tablespoons butter, melted

1 cup raspberries

1 cup blackberries

Whipped cream

Preheat grill to medium heat. Brush both sides of the pound cake slices with melted butter. Grill until just toasted, 1 to 2 minutes per side. Top with berries and a dollop of whipped cream.

Serves 4-6

LIQUID BOURBON BALL

Bourbon ball candies are famous in Kentucky. They are made of chocolate and bourbon with a nut either on top or in the center. This cocktail is a liquid version of the popular candy and often those who do not like bourbon do enjoy this cocktail.

In a shaker with ice, add:
2 ounces Woodford Reserve bourbon
1 ounce dark crème de cocoa
½ ounce walnut liqueur (or your favorite nut liqueur)

Shake and strain into a martini glass.

Top with ice chards from the shaker, as an option.

ITALIAN CUPCAKES

CUPCAKES:

15.25-ounce package yellow cake mix

3.4-ounce package instant vanilla pudding mix

3 eggs

½ cup vegetable oil

1 cup Tuaca Italian liqueur

GLAZE:

4 cups confectioners' sugar

¼ cup fresh lemon juice

1 lemon, zested, ½ reserved for garnish

2 tablespoons vegetable oil

¼ cup Tuaca Italian liqueur

Preheat oven to 325 degrees.

Grease miniature muffin tins with oil or baking spray. Beat the cake mix, pudding mix, eggs, oil and Tuaca in a large bowl on low for 30 seconds, then on high for 2 minutes. Pour the batter into the muffin tins. Bake for 10-12 minutes. Turn out onto the counter and cool slightly.

To make the glaze: Sift the sugar into a large bowl then add the lemon juice, ½ of the lemon zest, oil and Tuaca. Mix until smooth. While still warm, dip the cupcakes into the glaze. Place on wire racks with paper underneath to catch the drips.

Garnish with the remaining lemon zest, then store in air-tight containers.

Makes 48

HOT APPLE PIE

This cocktail tastes as if you are drinking a liquid apple pie. It is delicious in the fall, winter or over the holidays when apple cider is in season. For a party, you can multiply the recipe and serve the drink from a coffee urn. It will remain hot and guests can serve themselves. Offer whipped cream as an additional topper.

In a mug, add:
4 ounces hot apple cider
2 ounces Tuaca Italian liqueur

Garnish with a cinnamon stick and dash of cinnamon.

APPLE CINNAMON ENCHILADAS

2 teaspoons sugar
½ teaspoon cinnamon
1 20-ounce can apple pie filling
8 6-inch flour tortillas
2 tablespoons butter, melted
Caramel syrup
Whipped cream or ice cream (optional)

Preheat oven to 350 degrees.

In a small bowl, combine the sugar and cinnamon.

Spoon the pie filling evenly onto the center of each tortilla. Roll tortillas and place seam side down on a lightly greased baking pan. Brush each roll with melted butter and bake for 20 minutes. Sprinkle with the cinnamon sugar mixture and let cool, slightly. Cut each roll in half, drizzle with caramel syrup and serve with whipped cream or ice cream, if desired.

Serves 8

Note: You can also use cherry or peach pie filling.

FROZEN GRASSHOPPER

In a blender, add:

3 cups ice

4 ounces green crème de menthe

4 ounces white crème de cacao

1 pint vanilla ice cream

Blend until frothy. Pour into cocktail glasses and garnish with mint sprigs.

Serves 8

BRANDY ALEXANDER

In a shaker with ice, add:

1½ ounces brandy

1 ounce dark crème de cacao

1 ounce half & half

Shake and strain into a glass and garnish with grated nutmeg.

GIN

Gin, which can be traced back to the Middle Ages, was created by a Dutch physician and was first used for medicinal purposes. Its flavor is primarily derived from juniper berries and other herbs and spices. The Dutch word jenever translates to juniper.

As the spirit became more refined and was used more for drinking than for medicinal purposes, the English adopted it as the spirit of choice. One of the most popular drinks, gin and tonic, was created by adding gin to quinine. The British colonies used quinine as an effective anti-malarial compound and dissolved it in carbonated water to form tonic water. The gin, as they say, "helped the medicine go down."

Today, only a small amount of quinine is found in tonic water. During the Prohibition era, many secretly produced what was called "bathtub gin," which was available in speakeasies. After Prohibition, gin continued its popularity in many cocktails, especially in the classic martini, which was made with gin and not vodka.

Here's to seeing you in a nearby gin joint or mill.

Cheers!

RAMOS GIN FIZZ

This New Orleans classic was invented in the 1880s by Henry C. Ramos, "A Gentleman among Bartenders." This cocktail needs to be well shaken to be made correctly. There is a blind shake (without ice) and then a traditional shake (with ice). The Ramos Gin Fizz is still easily found in New Orleans and many fine establishments in the South.

In a shaker without ice, add:

1½ ounces gin

1 tablespoon Simple Syrup (page 202)

½ ounce fresh lemon juice

½ ounce fresh lime juice

1 fresh egg white (pasteurized, if you prefer)

1 ounce heavy cream

3 drops orange flower water

Shake vigorously to combine ingredients. Add ice to the shaker and shake again for a minute (more if you have it in you). Strain into a tall glass.

Top with 1 ounce club soda, stir and garnish with an orange slice.

Note: Look for orange flower water in well-stocked liquor, cooking and grocery stores, or order it online. Instead of using this, you can substitute a little grated orange zest.

NEGRONI

This classic Italian cocktail is now being served in a variety of bars and restaurants and is a nice sipping drink or a perfect aperitif. It can be an acquired taste, but it is worth a try – several times!

In an old-fashioned glass with ice, add:

1 ounce gin
1 ounce sweet vermouth
1 ounce Campari

Stir well and garnish with a silver-dollar-size slice of orange peel.

Note: Before garnishing, squeeze the peel over the drink to release the oils.

BENEDICTINE BACON TOASTS

1 English (seedless) cucumber, peeled
1 medium onion
2 8-ounce packages cream cheese, softened
2-3 drops green food coloring
Dash of hot sauce

1 pound bacon, cooked crisp, crumbled
1 loaf whole wheat bread, sliced

To make the Benedictine: grate the cucumber and onion (easiest with a food processor). Drain well by placing in a strainer and pressing down with a spoon to remove all of the liquid. In a small bowl or food processor, add the cucumber and onion, cream cheese, food coloring and hot sauce. Mix well, until combined.

Lightly toast the bread slices then, using a cookie cutter or the top of a jar, stamp out 1½-inch bread rounds. You can usually get 3 rounds per slice of bread. Spread a generous amount of the Benedictine on a bread round, then dip it in the bacon pieces. They will stick to the bread. Repeat the steps for each bread round.

Serves 8-10

THE CLASSIC MARTINI

The original martini was made with gin and dry vermouth. Eventually, the martini moved into the vodka category and became drier and drier, leaving out most or all of the vermouth. I recommend you use vermouth and garnish your martini with olives.

Note: Blue cheese, almond, anchovy and other stuffed olives are also delicious in this cocktail. Some people like their martinis slightly "dirty," which means adding a little olive juice.

Be sure to have your martini glass and garnishes well-chilled so they do not warm up the drink. Stir your martini aggressively to dilute some of the ice to soften the drink.

In a mixing glass with ice, add:
2 ounces gin
¾ ounce dry vermouth

Stir for at least 30 seconds, strain into a well-chilled martini glass, then garnish with olives.

Note: I prefer the French vermouth, Noilly Prat.

FRENCH INVASION

In a tall glass with ice, add:
1½ ounces gin
½ ounce elderflower liqueur
3 ounces tonic water
Squeeze of lime

Stir and garnish with a lime wedge.

Note: If you make tonic water ice cubes, your drink will not dilute as the ice melts. This is a good trick for gin and tonics as well.

BLUE CHEESE TOASTS

½ cup non-fat plain yogurt (preferably Greek-style)
½ cup mayonnaise
2 cloves garlic, crushed
½ teaspoon black pepper
1 cup parmesan cheese, freshly grated
1 cup blue cheese, crumbled
3 slices bacon, cooked crisp, crumbled
1 baguette, sliced into ½-inch rounds
½ cup green onions, finely chopped

Preheat oven to 400 degrees.

In a medium bowl, combine the yogurt, mayonnaise, garlic and pepper. Stir in the cheeses and bacon.

Spread 1 generous tablespoon of the cheese mixture on each bread round and place on a baking sheet. Bake until the cheese starts to melt and the bread is toasted, about 10 minutes.

Sprinkle with the green onions and serve warm.

Serves 8-10

BASIL BLING

Basil is a delicious accompaniment to gin. This cocktail is worth the muddling and fresh basil is a must.

In a mixing glass, add:
1 ounce fresh lemon juice
1 ounce Simple Syrup (page 202)
5 basil leaves

Muddle the above, then add 2 ounces gin and ice.

Shake and strain into a chilled martini glass. Garnish with a basil leaf.

GT RAZZ

In a rocks glass with ice, add:

1½ ounces gin

¾ ounce Chambord liqueur

3 ounces tonic water

Splash of bitters

Squeeze of lime

Stir and garnish with raspberries.

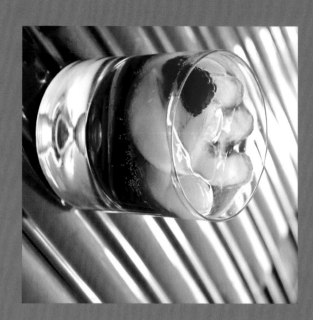

SHRIMP MOUSSE

2 green onions, roughly chopped

4 ounces cream cheese, softened

2 tablespoons lemon juice

1 teaspoon seafood seasoning, plus more for garnish

1 pound cooked shrimp, peeled, deveined

1 English (seedless) cucumber, sliced into ¼-inch rounds

Add the green onions, cream cheese, lemon juice and seasoning to a food processor or blender. Pulse to combine, then add the shrimp and pulse to finish combining.

Arrange the cucumber slices on a serving platter and place a dollop of the mousse on each slice or use a piping bag for a prettier look. Top with a sprinkling of additional seafood seasoning and refrigerate until serving.

Serves 8-10

MOCKTAILS

One of the best tips in hosting a cocktail and appetizer party is to offer plenty of alcohol-free choices. I always have a signature cocktail and an alcohol-free version or "mocktail" available. These are served in the same glass with the same garnish so everyone feels part of the party. Responsible hosting is a hallmark and really shows you are a true professional and genuinely care about your guests and their needs. Spice simple alcohol-free choices up with fun flavors and garnishes. You want to make these cocktails as festive and fun as those with a spirit or wine.

Cheers!

SUMMER HEAT

In a shaker with ice, add:
¼ jalapeño pepper, sliced into rounds, seeds removed
4 ounces lemonade
2 drops raspberry syrup

Shake and strain into a tall glass with ice.
Garnish with a jalapeño pepper.

WINTER WARMER

In a mug with 6 ounces hot cocoa, add peppermint syrup to taste.

Garnish with peppermint sticks.

ROASTED GARLIC DIP

12 bulbs garlic
¼ cup olive oil, plus more, as needed
8 3-inch sprigs fresh rosemary, more for garnish
½ cup parmesan cheese, grated
½ teaspoon Kosher salt
½ teaspoon black pepper
30 Filo dough cups

Preheat oven to 350 degrees.

Slice the tops off the garlic bulbs to expose the cloves. Place on a large sheet of aluminum foil on a baking sheet. Pour the olive oil over the cut garlic and place the rosemary on top. Make a tent with the foil, sealing in the garlic.

Bake for 45 minutes, until the garlic is soft. When cool, remove and discard the rosemary, then squeeze the garlic cloves into a food processor. If necessary, add a little olive oil to process into a paste. Add the cheese, salt and pepper.

Serve warm or at room temperature in Filo cups or with crusty bread. Garnish with chopped fresh rosemary.

Serves 10-12

Note: You can use the already-peeled cloves of garlic in this recipe. Just substitute 4 cups garlic cloves for the 12 bulbs.

RASPBERRY-MINT SMASH

In a mixing glass, add:
8 raspberries
6 mint leaves
2 ounces ginger beer

Muddle the raspberries, mint and ginger beer.

Then, add an additional 4 ounces of ginger beer and stir.

Strain into a rocks glass with ice.

Garnish with a mint sprig.

BRUSCHETTA

1 baguette, cut into ½-inch-thick slices
2 tablespoons olive oil, plus more, as needed
2 cloves garlic, halved, plus 2 more, minced
4 ounces goat cheese, softened
6 Roma tomatoes, seeded, chopped
Kosher salt
Black pepper
3 tablespoons fresh basil, thinly sliced
Capers

Preheat oven to 325 degrees.

Arrange the bread on a baking sheet and brush each side with olive oil. Bake the bread until toasted, about 4 minutes per side. While still warm, rub cut sides of garlic over one side of the toast then top with a smear of goat cheese

In a small bowl, combine the tomatoes, minced garlic and 1 tablespoon olive oil. Season with salt and pepper.

Top each toast with the tomato mixture, capers and basil.

Serves 6-8

Note: For a smoky flavor try grilling the bread.

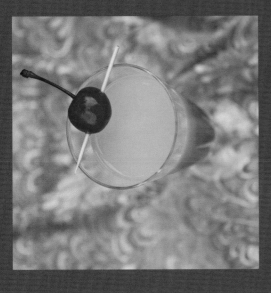

FLORIDA SUNSET

In tall narrow glass, add:
4 ounces orange juice, chilled
1 ounce grenadine syrup, chilled
Top with club soda, chilled
Garnish with a maraschino cherry

Note: To layer this drink, add the orange juice, then add the grenadine, slowly pouring over the back of a spoon.

ISLAND COOLER

In a shaker with ice, add:
3 ounces coconut water
2 ounces pineapple juice

Shake and strain into a martini glass rimmed
with macadamia nuts.
Garnish with a pineapple wedge.

*Note: To rim the glass, dip the outside edge of the
glass in a plate of honey, then in a plate of crushed
macadamia nuts.*

CRAB DEVILED EGGS

8 large eggs, hard-boiled, peeled

3 tablespoons non-fat plain yogurt (preferably Greek-style)

1 tablespoon shallot, finely chopped

1 tablespoon fresh lemon juice

1 tablespoon fresh tarragon, finely chopped

½ teaspoon hot sauce

8 ounces crabmeat

Kosher salt

Black pepper

Paprika, for garnish

Cut the eggs in half lengthwise. Scoop out the yolks of 5 eggs (reserve the rest for another use) into a medium-size bowl. Mash with a fork, and then mix in the yogurt, shallot, lemon juice, tarragon and hot sauce. Add the crabmeat, then season to taste with salt and pepper.

Mound the crab mixture into the 16 egg-white halves and garnish with paprika.

Serves 6-8

Note: The crab mixture can be made 6 hours ahead. Cover and refrigerate until ready to assemble and serve.

BLACKBERRY BOUNCE

In a mixing glass, add:
8 blackberries
Squeeze of lime

Muddle the blackberries.
Then, add 6 ounces blueberry juice and stir.

Pour into a rocks glass and top with club soda.
Garnish with a lime wedge and blackberries.

Note: If you wish, you can strain out the crushed blackberries.

PUNCHES AND PITCHERS

Punch was introduced to England from India and dates back to the early 17th century. The word *punch* derived from the Hindi word panch, which means five, because the drink was originally made with five ingredients: alcohol, sugar, lemon, water, and tea or spices.

In colonial America, inns would serve a house punch to patrons and overnight guests. Punches became popular for parties as well, because they were easy to make and served many people. The punch bowl became a place to gather and socialize. Traditionally, small mugs were used for punch so they could be refilled often, offering people another chance to gather around the punch bowl for more socializing.

Punches are, once again, making their way back into the party scene. Pitchers are also a great way to serve punches if you don't want to bring out a big punch bowl.

Cheers!

PUNCH ROYAL

In a punch bowl or large pitcher, add:

8 ounces Chambord liqueur
8 ounces cranberry juice, chilled
2 750-ml bottles Korbel Brut California Champagne, chilled

Stir and garnish with fresh raspberries or blackberries, then serve immediately.

Note: For a dramatic look, use a small Bundt mold to freeze water and raspberries and float the ice with berries in the punch.

PROSCIUTTO SALAD BITES

6 8½-inch diameter rice paper rounds
18 thin slices prosciutto
9 large romaine lettuce leaves, sliced lengthwise, spine removed
Ranch salad dressing
¼ cup Panko bread crumbs, toasted

Serves 8-10

Pour warm water into a pie plate, filling it halfway. Submerge 1 rice paper round in the water until it begins to soften, about 45 seconds. Place the rice paper on a kitchen towel and top with 2-3 slices of prosciutto, covering most of the rice paper.

Place 3 lettuce slices in the front ⅓ of the roll. Starting with the lettuce closest to you, roll into a cylinder, enclosing filling. Wrap in plastic. Repeat with remaining rounds and filling. Chill for up to 3 hours.

Remove the plastic wrap from the rolls, trim ends, then cut each roll into 5 pieces and stand upright on a platter. Top with a dollop of the salad dressing and bread crumbs.

SWEET BOURBON PUNCH

In a punch bowl or large pitcher, add:

16 ounces unsweetened iced tea

1 cup superfine sugar

1 12-ounce can frozen orange juice

1 12-ounce can frozen limeade

1 750-ml bottle Old Forester bourbon

7 cups water

Stir, then chill until served. Garnish with sliced lemons, limes and oranges.

Serving idea: Instead of using punch glasses, serve in small canning jars.

APPLE AND GOAT CHEESE TARTS

2 sheets frozen puff pastry, thawed according to directions on the package

10 ounces goat cheese, softened

3 red apples, cored, thinly sliced into 36 pieces

2 tablespoons extra virgin olive oil

2 tablespoons fresh thyme leaves

Kosher salt

Black pepper

Preheat oven to 400 degrees.

Cut each sheet into 9 3-inch squares, then cut each square diagonally to make 18 triangles per sheet. Top each triangle with cheese and an apple slice, then brush with olive oil. Sprinkle with thyme, salt and pepper.

Bake on a lightly greased baking sheet for 20 minutes or until the pastry is cooked through and lightly browned. Serve immediately.

Serves 10-12

PARTY PUNCH

In a punch bowl or large pitcher, add:

16 ounces Herradura Silver tequila

2 cups fresh lime juice

2½ cups pineapple juice

Stir, then chill until served. Garnish with pineapple rings and serve with pineapple wedges on the glasses.

LEMON–LIME SPARKLER

In a punch bowl or large pitcher, add:

1 12-ounce can frozen pink lemonade
1 12-ounce can frozen limeade
2 750-ml bottles Korbel Brut
    California Champagne, chilled

Stir and garnish with honeydew melon balls
and mint, then serve immediately.

SUNSHINE PUNCH

In a punch bowl or large pitcher, add:

1 750-ml bottle Southern Comfort
6 ounces fresh lemon juice
1 6-ounce can frozen lemonade
1 6-ounce can frozen orange juice
3 liters lemon-lime soda, chilled

Stir and garnish with lemons and limes, then
serve immediately.

BUFFALO CHICKEN SALAD SLIDERS

Everyone loves Buffalo Chicken Wings. Make them easier to eat (without the bones) by combining all of the traditional ingredients into a slider.

4 cups chicken, cooked, shredded
1 cup celery, finely chopped
½ cup hot wing sauce
½ cup blue cheese dressing
½ cup crumbled blue cheese
12 slider buns

In a large bowl, combine the chicken, celery, wing sauce and blue cheese dressing.
Top each bun with the salad mixture and add a sprinkle of blue cheese.

Makes 12

Note: Pick up a cooked rotisserie chicken to make this recipe even easier to make.

MARGARITAS FOR MANY

This is a delicious, easy-to-make drink, loved by everyone and perfect for large parties.

In a large punch bowl or pitcher, add:

1 1.75-liter bottle tequila

2 12-ounce cans frozen lemonade

1 12-ounce can frozen limeade

1 gallon water

Stir, then chill until served. Salt the rims of the glasses and garnish with a lime wheel.

Note: You can add this to a blender with ice for a frozen version or add your favorite juice, nectar or syrup to add additional flavor. For example, add a little pomegranate juice and you have a pomegranate margarita.

RUM

Rum is a distilled spirit made from sugar cane or from the by-product of making sugar, molasses. Many types of rum are aged in oak barrels after being distilled. Most of the rum production in the world occurs in the Caribbean or Latin America. Many people don't know that rum fostered the slave trade and actually perpetuated the American Revolution. Rum is also featured in folklore, as it is the spirit associated with pirates who sailed the Caribbean. So, yo, ho, ho and a bottle of rum!

Cheers!

DAIQUIRI

The daiquiri was one of Ernest Hemingway's favorite cocktails. He preferred to leave out most of the sugar, however. This is the classic recipe, which is fresh and only has three ingredients. Many have added additional fruits and sweeteners but this is the original recipe from Cuba. Adjust this cocktail to your liking by adding or subtracting lime juice and Simple Syrup.

In a shaker with ice, add:

2 ounces light rum

¾ ounce fresh lime juice

¾ ounce Simple Syrup (page 202)

Shake and strain into a chilled cocktail glass. Garnish with a lime wedge.

CARIBBEAN PORK TENDERLOIN

¼ cup dark rum
¼ cup soy sauce
¼ cup brown sugar, packed
3 cloves garlic, minced
1 8-ounce can pineapple, crushed
1 teaspoon fresh ginger, grated, or ¼ teaspoon ground ginger
1 teaspoon Worcestershire sauce
¼ cup vegetable oil
2 1-pound pork tenderloins
1 baguette, sliced
Pineapple salsa

Combine rum, soy sauce, brown sugar, garlic, pineapple, ginger, Worcestershire sauce and oil in a large bowl. Whisk until brown sugar has dissolved. Set aside ½ cup for basting.

Place marinade and pork tenderloins in a zip-top plastic bag and place in the refrigerator overnight.

Bring to room temperature. Grill over medium-high heat or bake at 350 degrees for approximately 15-25 minutes. Baste often while cooking. Pork should reach 165 degrees internally.

To serve, place pork tenderloin medallions on baguette slices and top with pineapple salsa.

Serves 10-12

DARK AND STORMY

If you go or have ever been to Bermuda, a Dark and Stormy is the drink to order. Here is the famous recipe to enjoy at home.

In a tall glass with ice, add:
1½ ounces Goslings dark rum (or other dark rum if you can't find the Bermuda original)
4 ounces ginger beer
Squeeze of lime

Stir and garnish with a lime wedge.

BLUE WAVE

In a snifter or rocks glass with ice, add:

1½ ounces rum
1 ounce blue Curacao
2 ounces pineapple juice
2 ounces cranberry juice

Stir and garnish with a
pineapple wedge.

CARIBBEAN COOLER

In a shaker with ice, add:

1½ ounces light rum
3 ounces pineapple juice
2 ounces guava juice
Squeeze of lime

Shake and strain into a rocks glass with ice.
Garnish with a dash of nutmeg and a cherry.

MAI TAI

Yes, they do taste better in Hawaii, but you can bring the Islands home with this recipe.

In a shaker with ice, add:

1 ounce light rum
1 ounce dark rum
3 ounces pineapple juice
2 ounces orange juice
1 teaspoon grenadine syrup
1 teaspoon almond syrup

Shake and strain into a rocks glass with ice. Garnish with a pineapple wedge.

MANGO SHRIMP SALSA

1 mango, peeled, pitted, diced
1 red pepper, seeded, diced
1 jalapeño, seeded, diced
¼ cup red onion, diced
2 tablespoons garlic, minced
2 tablespoons cilantro, chopped
½ pound cooked shrimp, chopped
⅛ cup fresh orange juice
⅛ cup fresh lime juice
Kosher salt
Black pepper

In a bowl, combine the mango, red pepper, jalapeño, onion, garlic, cilantro and shrimp. Stir in the orange and lime juice and season with salt and pepper.

Refrigerate for 1 hour. Serve with tortilla chips.

Serves 6-8

ISLAND MUSSELS

2 pounds mussels, cleaned

1 tablespoon olive oil

2 tablespoons shallot, finely chopped

6 cloves garlic, minced

1 teaspoon fresh ginger, grated

½ cup light rum

½ cup water

1 lime, juiced

Pinch red pepper flakes

1 teaspoon fresh basil, finely chopped

2 tablespoons unsalted butter

Chives, finely chopped, for garnish

1 baguette, sliced and grilled

Discard any mussels with broken shells. Heat oil in a large stockpot, then sauté the shallot, garlic and ginger. Add the mussels and stir. Add the rum, water, lime juice and red pepper flakes. Cover the pot and steam over medium-high heat for 5 minutes or until the mussels open. Stir in the basil and butter, cover the pot, and steam for another minute.

Ladle mussels and broth into shallow bowls and top with chives. Serve with grilled bread.

Serves 4

HOT BUTTERED RUM

This is a wonderful drink to enjoy on a cold night.

1 teaspoon butter
1 teaspoon brown sugar
1 dash cinnamon
1 dash nutmeg
1½ ounces rum
3 ounces hot water

In a glass mug, add the butter, sugar, cinnamon and nutmeg.

Pour in the rum and hot water.

Stir well and garnish with a dash more of cinnamon.

SKINNY COCKTAILS

Everyone is trying to cut calories these days, any way they can. This is easy to do when it comes to cocktails and mixers. There are now many choices in the mixer world. Several have perfected their flavors and do not have that "chemical" taste they have had in the past.

My favorites include Ocean Spray "Light" and "Diet" juice mixers. Ocean Spray offers a wide variety of juices and blends which mix well with spirits. Finest Call and Master of Mixes also have a great variety of lower-calorie and sugar-free offerings. Their "Lite" sweet and sour and margarita mixes are just a couple of examples of the many they make. They even offer Lite Strawberry Daiquiri Mix and Lite Simple Syrup which have the proper viscosity, ensuring that your cocktails have the right mouthfeel.

A wide variety of powdered calorie-free mixes are now available, and they work well in cocktails. I have also discovered flavored drops, like those by Dasani, which add easy, calorie-free flavors to cocktails.

Another tip in saving calories is to lower the amount of alcohol in a cocktail. For example, instead of a 1½-ounce pour, consider a 1-ounce pour per cocktail.

Cheers!

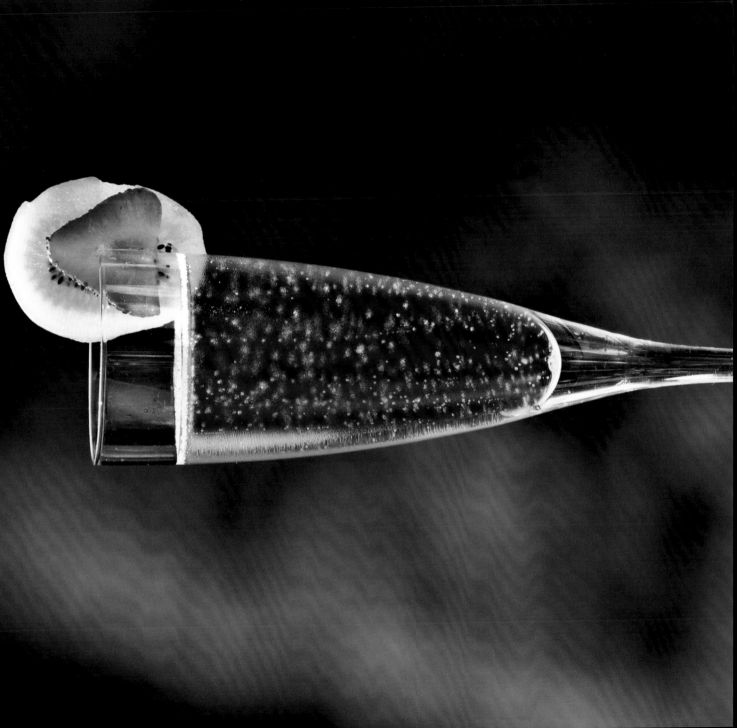

RITA'S DE-LITE

In a glass with crushed ice, add:
1 ounce blanco tequila
4 ounces light margarita mix
Squeeze of lime

Stir and garnish with a lime wheel.

BLUEBERRY BLING

In a tall glass with ice, add:
1 ounce vodka
4 ounces diet blueberry juice

Stir and garnish with fresh blueberries.

THYME-TINI

In a shaker with ice, add:

1 ounce vodka
4 thyme sprigs (bruise by squeezing them between your hands)
3 ounces sugar-free lemonade

Shake and strain into a martini glass. Garnish with a thyme sprig.

STRAWBERRY-KIWI SPARKLER

In a tall flute, add:

4 ounces Korbel Brut California Champagne
Several drops strawberry kiwi flavored drops, such as Dasani

Garnish with slice of kiwi and strawberry.

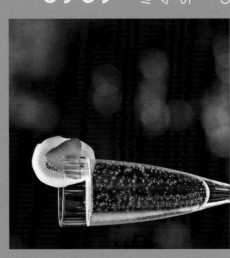

AHI TUNA BITES

Ahi tuna, sushi grade
Extra virgin olive oil
Cracked black peppercorns
Plain rice crackers
Teriyaki sauce
Wasabi caviar

Brush all four sides of the tuna with extra virgin olive oil. Then, coat all sides with cracked black peppercorns, pressing them into the tuna so they stick.

Sear the tuna for 1 minute per side in a hot skillet. Let rest for 1 hour in the refrigerator or until ready to serve.

Cut the tuna into ¼-inch slices. Put a small amount of teriyaki sauce on a rice cracker, then top with a slice of tuna and a dollop of caviar.

Serves 6-8

Note: Buy sushi-grade Ahi tuna from your favorite fish monger and have it cut into 1-inch diameter logs.

FRESCA CHILL

In a rocks glass with ice, add:

1 ounce vodka

4 ounces Fresca

Splash of diet cranberry juice

Stir and garnish with a slice of lime.

PEA SOUP

1 tablespoon unsalted butter

2 cups leeks, chopped

1 cup yellow onion, chopped

4 cups low-sodium chicken broth

2 10-ounce packages frozen peas

¼ cup fresh mint leaves, chopped

1 teaspoon Kosher salt

½ teaspoon ground black pepper

Non-fat plain yogurt (preferably Greek-style), for garnish

Chopped chives, for garnish

Hot sauce, for garnish

Heat the butter in a large saucepan. Add the leeks and onion, then cook over medium-low heat for 8-10 minutes, until the onions are soft. Add the chicken broth. Increase the heat to high, and bring to a boil. Add the peas and cook for 3-5 minutes, until the peas are tender. Remove from the heat and add the mint, salt, and pepper.

Purée the soup in batches. Place 2 cups of soup in a blender, purée on low speed. Hot liquids expand so be careful, put a kitchen towel over the blender lid for safety. Pour the soup into a large bowl and repeat until all of the soup is puréed. Pour the soup into serving dishes or mini martini glasses and top with yogurt, chives and hot sauce.

Serves 6

Note: This soup can be served hot or cold.

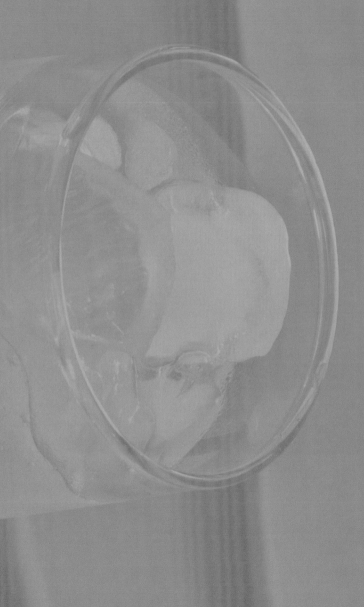

SCARLETT'S SECRET

In a tall glass with ice, add:

1 ounce Southern Comfort

3 ounces diet cranberry juice

Squeeze of lime

Stir and garnish with a lime wedge.

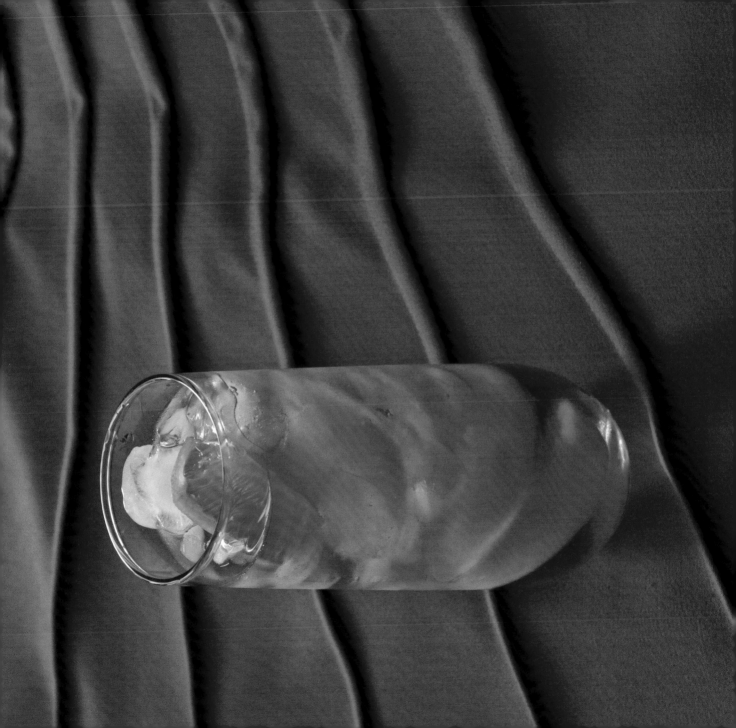

SMOKED SALMON FLATBREAD

½ cup non-fat plain yogurt (preferably Greek-style)
1 tablespoon red onion, finely chopped
1 tablespoon horseradish
1 teaspoon fresh dill, finely chopped, plus sprigs for garnish
Pinch of Kosher salt
Pinch of black pepper

4 pita bread rounds
16 ounces smoked salmon

In a small bowl, combine the yogurt, onion, horseradish, dill, salt and pepper. Cover each pita bread round with 4 ounces of smoked salmon.

Cut each round in half, then in half again, then cut each quarter to make 8 triangles. Top each triangle with a dollop of sauce and garnish with a dill sprig.

Serves 10-12

SOUTHERN STRAWBERRY

In a blender with 2 cups ice, add:

1 ounce Southern Comfort

5 ounces light strawberry daiquiri mix

Blend until smooth, and garnish with a strawberry.

TEQUILA

Tequila is gaining in popularity as people become more educated about the category. The spirit dates back to the 16th century and was said to be created by accident. Supposedly, a lightning strike hit an agave plant and cooked it. The cooked agave had a wonderful smell and taste, similar to cooked sweet potatoes. It then fermented naturally from wild yeast spores in the air. The Aztecs drank this concoction and called it Pulque. When the Spaniards arrived, they began to distill the fermented beverage and created the first indigenous North American distilled spirit, tequila.

Tequila is produced exclusively in what is known as the tequila region, found mostly in the state of Jalisco. There are two categories of tequila – mixtos and 100% agave. Mixtos use no less than 51% agave, with other sugars making up the remainder. The 100% agave does not add any additional sugars.

Contrary to what most people think, the agave plant is not related to the cactus but is a succulent, related to the aloe plant.

Tequila is bottled in one of five categories:

1. **Blanco:** Meaning "white" or "silver," Blanco is un-aged or aged up to less than two months. This style of tequila shows off the wonderful spicy qualities of the agave plant.
2. **Gold:** Usually a mixto, Gold refers to the caramel coloring added to give this tequila a gold color.
3. **Reposado:** Meaning "rested," Reposado is aged a minimum of two months, but less than one year, in oak barrels. This style of tequila exhibits some vanilla and spice flavors through its oak barrel aging.
4. **Anejo:** Meaning "aged," Anejo spends a minimum of one year, but less than three years, in small oak barrels. This style of tequila brings in more flavors from the barrel, such as more vanilla and cinnamon.
5. **Extra Anejo:** Meaning "extra aged," Extra Anejo is aged a minimum of three years in oak barrels. This category of tequila was established in 2006 by Casa Herradura. It is a luxuriously easy-to-drink tequila, and is reminiscent of fine Cognacs.

Look for 100% blue agave and try all of the expressions above. You will find each one has its special place in the tequila category.

Salud!

PALOMA

In Mexico, the favorite drink among locals is the Paloma. It is made with el Jimador Reposado tequila and grapefruit soda, with a pinch of salt and squeeze of lime. For a lighter version, I use Fresca.

In a tall glass with ice, add:

1½ ounces el Jimador Reposado tequila

4 ounces Fresca

Pinch of salt

Squeeze of lime

Stir and garnish with a slice of lime.

JALISCO SUNRISE

In a shaker with ice, add:

1½ ounces el Jimador Blanco tequila

2 ounces pineapple juice

2 ounces cranberry juice

Squeeze of lime

Shake and strain into a rocks glass with ice. Garnish with an orange slice and a cherry.

CORN WITH TEQUILA LIME DRESSING

4 cups cooked corn kernels, fresh or frozen

1 cup red bell pepper, diced

1 tablespoon olive oil

1 tablespoon tequila

1 tablespoon agave nectar

½ lime, juiced

1 clove garlic, minced

¼ teaspoon Kosher salt

¼ teaspoon black pepper

2 tablespoons fresh cilantro, finely chopped

In a medium-size bowl, combine the corn and red pepper.

In a small bowl, whisk together the olive oil, tequila, agave nectar, lime juice, garlic, salt, and pepper. Pour the dressing over the corn and pepper mixture. Stir in the cilantro and adjust the seasoning, as needed. Cover and chill for 1 hour.

Serves 6

Note: This is an excellent side dish or salsa served with tortilla chips.

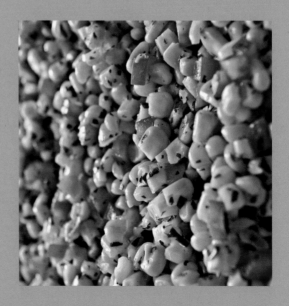

2-1-1 MARGARITA

The best margarita is made with just three ingredients: a good tequila, fresh lime juice, and agave nectar. Agave nectar is syrup which is made from the same plant used to make tequila. Fortunately, agave nectar is now widely distributed and can be found in most grocery stores. Prior, it could only be found in health food stores because of its health benefits, like being lower in sugar than other sweeteners. You will always remember the formula if you think of 2-1-1.

In a shaker with ice, add:

2 ounces Herradura Reposado tequila

1 ounce Agave Syrup (page 203)

1 ounce fresh lime juice

Shake and strain into a glass with crushed ice. Garnish with a lime wheel.

CUCUMBER SMASH

Cucumber in a cocktail adds a clean and refreshing taste, especially when paired with tequila. I recommend using English cucumbers because they have a thin skin (no need to peel), are seedless and muddle easily.

In a mixing glass, add:
1½ ounces blanco tequila
3 ¼-inch slices cucumber

Muddle the cucumber and tequila, then add:
3 ounces lemonade

Shake and strain into a rocks glass with ice. Garnish with a cucumber slice.

Note: You can leave the muddled cucumber in the cocktail or use a strainer to remove it.

GRILLED GUACAMOLE

4 avocados, ripe but firm, halved, pits removed

Olive oil

½ lime, juiced

Kosher salt

Fresh ground black pepper

¼ cup red onion, finely chopped (optional)

2 tablespoons cilantro, finely chopped (optional)

Dash of hot sauce (optional)

Tortilla chips

Heat a gas or charcoal grill to medium heat. Lightly brush each avocado half with oil. Grill, cut-side-down, until marks appear and the avocados are heated through, about 5 minutes. Take off the grill and let cool slightly.

Scoop out the insides into a bowl and mash with a fork. Stir in the lime juice and salt and pepper to taste. Add onion, cilantro and hot sauce, if you wish.

Serve immediately with chips.

Serves 4–6

Note: Grilling the avocados will help ripen them and turn the flesh a deep green color.

SWEET HEAT

"Salty and sweet" are a tasty combination which most people really love. Add a little heat to the "salty and sweet" and you get "sweet heat." Adjust the sweetness and heat levels to your own preference.

In a shaker with ice, add:

1½ ounces el Jimador Reposado tequila

3 ¼-inch slices jalapeño pepper (remove seeds and membrane for less heat)

1 ounce Honey Syrup (page 203)

3 ounces lemonade

Shake and strain into a cocktail glass rimmed with Sweet Heat Spice. Garnish with a jalapeño pepper slice.

SWEET HEAT SPICE

In a small bowl, add one part chili powder, one part sugar and one-half part Kosher salt. Rub lime around the rim of a cocktail glass and dip it in the spice mixture.

BEAN SALSA

1 15-ounce can black beans, drained, rinsed

1 15-ounce can pinto beans, drained, rinsed

1 10-ounce can chopped tomatoes and green chilies

½ cup cilantro, chopped

1 bunch green onions, chopped

1 teaspoon cumin

1 tablespoon olive oil

½ lime, juiced

½ teaspoon Kosher salt

½ teaspoon black pepper

Combine all ingredients in a large bowl. Serve with your favorite tortilla chips.

BIG BLUE AGAVE

In a glass with crushed ice, add:

1½ ounces Herradura Anejo tequila

3 ounces lemonade

½ ounce blue Curacao

Stir and garnish with an orange peel.

VODKA

Vodka is described as a neutral spirit which is a distillation of fermented substances, like grains, potatoes, or even fruits or sugar. Vodka dates back to the 1400s, and the debate whether it was created in Russia or Poland still continues today.

Vodka is one of the largest spirit categories. The number of vodkas available continues to grow, and there are countless flavor extensions added to vodka every day.

You might surprise yourself by taking a "blind" taste test to discover which vodka you like best. Often it is not the most expensive one you bought. The best way to tell if vodka has the true expression of a flavor is to use your nose to detect if the flavor you smell is true to the real fruit or to what is on the label. For example, grapefruit vodka should smell just like the zest of a real grapefruit.

At first, vodka had a hard time competing with the leading American spirit, gin. Two things really helped vodka take off as a spirit. The first was the Moscow Mule, a very easy drink to make, made with vodka, ginger beer and lime juice, served in a copper cup with crushed ice. The second was vodka's tagline, "It will leave you breathless," meaning that if you enjoyed a couple vodka drinks over lunch, the alcohol on your breath would not be detected.

Vodka is one of the most mixable spirits and can transform itself into many great cocktails. But you can also enjoy it like people do in Vodka-drinking nations like Russia, Poland and Finland and drink it chilled "neat."

Grab a vodka drink and say, Na zdrowie! Kippis! Cheers!

CAVIAR POTATOES

12 redskin potatoes, whole
Kosher salt
Black pepper
Sour cream
Caviar

Scrub the potatoes, then boil in salted water for 15-20 minutes or until fork tender. When cool, slice in half with a sharp knife, being careful not to tear the skin.

Using a melon baller or spoon, scoop out a small amount of potato from the cut side.

Season with salt and pepper, then place a dollop of sour cream and a small amount of caviar on top.

Serves 8-10

Note: Use your favorite caviar or a variety of types of caviar, including: paddlefish, sturgeon, lumpfish (black, red or gold), salmon or wasabi.

MANGO MOJITO

In a tall glass with ice, add:
2 ounces Finlandia Mango vodka
3 ounces Mint Simple Syrup (page 202)
½ ounce fresh lime juice
2 ounces club soda, chilled

Stir and garnish with a mint sprig.

FLEUR DE LIS

In a shaker with ice, add:

¾ ounce Chambord vodka
¾ ounce Chambord liqueur
2 ounces lemonade
1 ounce cranberry juice
Squeeze of lemon

Shake and strain into a rocks glass with ice.
Garnish with blackberries.

CITRUS SUNSHINE

In a tall glass with ice, add:

1½ ounces Finlandia Grapefruit vodka
1 ounce orange juice
3 ounces lemon-lime soda, chilled

Stir and garnish with a slice of lemon.

MOSCOW MULE

In a copper mug or rocks glass with crushed ice, add:

1½ ounces vodka
4 ounces ginger beer, chilled
Squeeze of lime

Stir and garnish with a lime wedge.

MANGO MOJO SCALLOPS

12 large sea scallops
2 teaspoons unsalted butter
2 teaspoons olive oil
Kosher salt
Black pepper
Mint leaves, for garnish

Using a paper towel, thoroughly pat the scallops dry, then season both sides with salt and pepper. Add the butter and oil to a sauté pan on high heat.

Sear the scallops on each side for 2 minutes until a golden crust forms. Place on serving spoons or a serving platter and top with a dollop of the mango sauce and a mint leaf.

For the sauce:
1 ripe mango, peeled, pitted, coarsely chopped
¼ cup Finlandia Mango vodka
¼ cup orange juice
¼ habanero or Scotch Bonnet pepper (seeds removed)

In a blender, purée the mango, vodka, orange juice and pepper until smooth.

Note: This sauce combines a cool combination of mango and a little heat with a sliver of pepper. The sauce is also delicious with chicken, firm whitefish or pork.

LYCHEE MARTINI

In a shaker with ice, add:
1½ ounces vodka
3 ounces lychee syrup

Shake and strain into a chilled martini glass.
Garnish with a lychee fruit.

FRENCH LEMONADE

In a tall glass with ice, add:

1½ ounces vodka

¾ ounce Chambord liqueur

¾ ounce elderflower liqueur

3 ounces lemonade

Stir and garnish with a lemon twist.

BIG CITY-TINI

In a shaker with ice, add:

1½ ounces Finlandia Grapefruit vodka

½ ounce orange liqueur

2 ounces white cranberry peach juice or white cranberry juice

Squeeze of lime

Shake and strain into a chilled cocktail glass. Garnish with a slice of grapefruit peel.

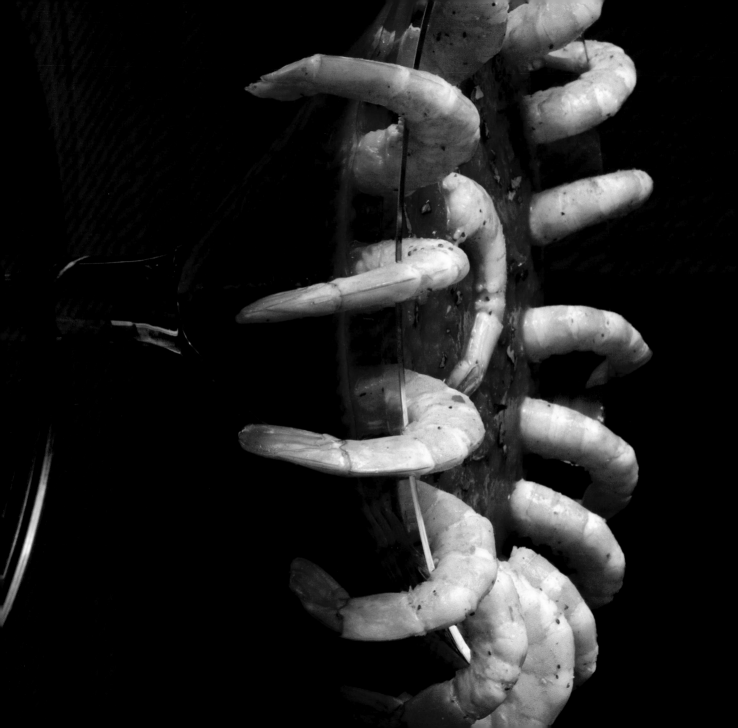

BLOODY MARY SHRIMP COCKTAIL

For the shrimp:
30 jumbo shrimp, cooked, peeled, deveined
1 lemon, cut in half
Seafood seasoning

Squeeze the lemon over the shrimp, then toss with seafood seasoning. Refrigerate until ready to serve.

For the sauce:
1 28-ounce can crushed tomatoes
2 tablespoons horseradish
2 tablespoons Worcestershire sauce
2 teaspoons hot sauce
½ lemon, juiced
½ cup celery, finely chopped
½ cup vodka, chilled

In a large bowl, combine the tomatoes, horseradish, Worcestershire, hot sauce, lemon juice, celery and vodka. Refrigerate until ready to serve.

To serve, pour the sauce into 6 chilled martini glasses and place 5 shrimp around the edge of each glass.

Serves 6

WHISKEY

The word whiskey comes from the Gaelic word for "water of life," or "whiskybae." The most noted whiskey-making countries include: Ireland, Scotland, Canada and the United States. Whiskey is spelled two ways, either whiskey or whisky. Ironically, countries with an "e" in their name, like America and Ireland, most commonly spell it Whiskey. Countries without an "e," like Scotland, Canada and Japan, spell it Whisky. Ultimately, distillers decide which spelling they prefer.

As America, the new world, was being settled, immigrants from Scotland and Ireland brought with them their whiskey-making talents and started producing whiskey with whatever grain they could find. Whiskey made its way across America as the west became settled, and many a cowboy would order a bottle or a shot of whiskey. No matter how you spell it, whiskeys make great cocktails.

Cheers!

WHISKEY SOUR

The quintessential whiskey drink is the Whiskey Sour. Unfortunately, this drink is too often made with low-quality whiskey, bad-tasting mixers and artificial foaming agents. To make this drink the correct way, you need a good quality whiskey, fresh lemon sour mix and egg white to create the foam. It needs to be blind-shaken (all ingredients in a shaker with no ice), and then shaken traditionally, with ice. To be safe, use pasteurized egg whites.

In a shaker, add:

1½ ounces Early Times Kentucky Whisky

2 ounces fresh lemon juice

1 ounce Simple Syrup (page 202)

1 teaspoon egg white

Shake vigorously, then add ice to shaker. Shake again, then pour the entire contents into a rocks glass. Garnish with an orange slice and a cherry.

CREAMY BACON DIP

8 ounces cream cheese, softened
2 cups sour cream
2 cups cheddar cheese, shredded, plus ½ cup
1 bunch green onions, chopped
½ cup cooked bacon, chopped
2 cloves garlic, minced
1 teaspoon horseradish
1 teaspoon Worcestershire sauce
Wheat crackers
Peppers, sliced wide for dipping

Preheat oven to 400 degrees.

In a large bowl, combine the cream cheese, sour cream, 2 cups cheese, green onions, bacon, garlic, horseradish and Worcestershire sauce. Spread into a 1-quart baking dish and top with the remaining ½ cup cheese.

Bake for 25-30 minutes until golden and bubbly. Serve immediately with crackers and sliced peppers.

Serves 8-10

BEE STING

In a tall glass with ice, add:

1½ ounces Jack Daniel's Tennessee Honey whiskey

4 ounces ginger beer

Squeeze of lime

Stir and garnish with a lime wheel.

TROPICAL JACK

In a shaker with ice, add:

1½ ounces Jack Daniel's Tennessee whiskey

2 ounces pineapple juice

1 ounce orange juice

Shake vigorously; the pineapple juice will create foam. Pour the entire contents into a rocks glass. Garnish with a pineapple wedge.

HURRICANE

This cocktail is a New Orleans favorite. If you don't have a hurricane glass, a tall glass will work just fine. You can also make this by the pitcher by adding equal parts of Southern Comfort, lemonade, orange juice and pineapple juice, with a splash of grenadine for color.

In a tall hurricane glass with ice, add:

1½ ounces Southern Comfort

1½ ounces lemonade

1½ ounces orange juice

1½ ounces pineapple juice

1 teaspoon grenadine

Stir and garnish with an orange slice and a cherry.

CHEESE BISCUITS

This is, by far, the best "cheese cookie" recipe I have ever tasted. Thank you to my good friend in the Deep South for sharing his once-secret recipe.

10 ounces sharp cheddar cheese, shredded
16 tablespoons (2 sticks) butter, softened
2 cups flour
½ teaspoon cayenne pepper
1½ cups Rice Krispies cereal
Garlic salt

Preheat oven to 375 degrees.

In a large bowl, using your hands, combine the cheese, butter, flour and pepper. Then add the cereal, until combined.

Break off a piece of dough and roll into a 1-inch diameter ball. Place on a non-stick baking sheet and mash with the tines of a fork. Repeat with the remaining dough.

Bake for 15 minutes, then sprinkle with garlic salt. Enjoy immediately or freeze in an air-tight container.

Makes 80

Note: Be sure to wash the baking sheet in between batches.

FRENCH CANADIAN COFFEE

In a mug of hot coffee, add:

1½ ounces Canadian Mist whisky

½ ounce Chambord liqueur

1 teaspoon maple syrup

Stir and top with whipped cream mixed with Chambord liqueur.

BBQ CHICKEN QUESADILLAS

4 cups chicken, cooked, shredded
1 cup BBQ sauce
1 tablespoon Jack Daniel's Tennessee Honey whiskey
8 8-inch flour tortillas
Vegetable oil
2 cups pepper jack cheese, shredded
Sour cream, for garnish
Jalapeños, sliced, for garnish
Green onions, chopped, for garnish

Preheat oven to 350 degrees.

In a medium bowl, combine the BBQ sauce and whiskey. Add the chicken and toss to coat.

Brush 4 tortillas with oil and place them oil side down on a baking sheet. Layer each tortilla with ¼ cup cheese, then 1 cup of chicken mixture, then another ¼ cup cheese. Top each with a tortilla, press to seal, then brush the top with oil.

Bake for 10 minutes, let cool slightly, then cut each quesadilla into 8 pieces. Garnish with sour cream, jalapeños and green onions.

Serves 14-16

Note: The BBQ chicken mixture is also delicious in tacos or on tortilla chips.

HOT TODDY

This classic cocktail will take the chill out on a cold night.

In a mug of hot water, add:

2 ounces whiskey

2 ounces Honey Syrup (page 203)

Squeeze of lemon

Stir and garnish with a lemon twist.

WINE COCKTAILS

The most widely known wine-based cocktails are sangrias, which come in red, white and sparkling varieties. There are many other wine-based cocktails that taste great and make for fun alternatives to standard beverage offerings. Champagne is a fantastic base for cocktails, as it adds a sparkling effervescence to every drink. Break out the wine and champagne and serve some of these festive cocktails at your next party.

Cheers!

SANGRIA SUNRISE

In a pitcher, add:
2 750-ml bottles of merlot or cabernet sauvignon wine
2 cups orange juice
6 ounces orange liqueur
2 ounces fresh lime juice

Stir, then chill until served. Garnish with sliced lemons, limes and oranges.

POM BEACH

In a shaker with ice, add:
3 ounces merlot or cabernet sauvignon wine
2 ounces pomegranate juice
1 ounce cranberry juice
Squeeze of lemon

Shake and strain into a wine glass. Garnish with a lemon twist

BLUE CHEESE GRAPES

5 ounces macadamia nuts, toasted, finely chopped

5 ounces pecans, toasted, finely chopped

5 ounces pistachios, toasted, finely chopped

8 ounces cream cheese, softened

8 ounces blue cheese, softened

2 tablespoons heavy cream

1 pound seedless grapes, washed, dried

Pour each type of nut into 3 separate bowls.

In a large bowl, add the cream cheese, blue cheese and cream, then beat until smooth. Put 5 grapes into the cheese mixture and stir by hand to coat each one. Roll the coated grapes in the toasted nuts and store on a tray lined with parchment paper. Repeat with the remaining grapes, cheese mixture and nuts.

You should end up with approximately 20 grapes rolled in each type of nut. Chill for up to 1 hour, then serve.

Serves 14-16

Note: Serve the grapes on a platter in the shape of a grape cluster, using grape leaves or flat-leaf parsley at the top of the "bunch."

MINI PIZZAS

Buy pre-made pizza dough, then build and bake your own mini pizzas. Roll out the dough, then stamp out 2-inch rounds using the top of a jar or cookie cutter. Add your favorite toppings and bake on a greased baking sheet at 450 degrees for 6-8 minutes.

Here are some of my favorite combinations:

Olive oil, pear, gorgonzola cheese, cracked black pepper

Olive oil, goat cheese, fresh fig

Olive oil, bacon, caramelized onion, sliced Gruyère cheese, fresh thyme

COOL BLUE

In a rocks glass with ice, add:
3 ounces Korbel Brut California Champagne
2 ounces lemonade
1 ounce blue Curaçao

Stir and garnish with an orange slice.

PINEAPPLE CRUSH

In a shaker with ice, add:

3 ounces Sonoma-Cutrer Sonoma Coast Chardonnay

2 ounces pineapple juice

1½ ounces orange juice

Shake and strain into a white wine glass.

Garnish with a pineapple wedge.

SPARKLING RASPBERRY

In a stemmed glass, add:

4 ounces Korbel Sweet Rose California Champagne, chilled

1 ounce Chambord vodka

2 ounces cranberry juice, chilled

Dash of bitters

Garnish with raspberries.

CHARDONNAY BELLINI

In a white wine glass, add:

4 ounces chardonnay, chilled

2 ounces peach nectar
(1 ounce, if using peach purée)

Top with Sprite

Stir and garnish with a peach slice.

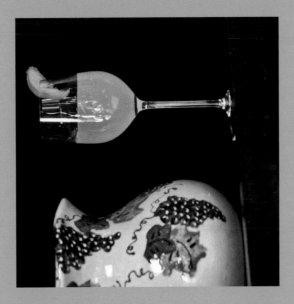

PÂTÉ AND GRAPES

Set out your favorite pâté, grapes and toasts to enjoy with your wine cocktails.

CHORIZO WITH RED WINE

1 pound chorizo sausage, cut into ¼-inch slices
½ cup cabernet sauvignon wine
2 tablespoons fresh parsley, chopped
2 cloves garlic, minced
1 baguette, cut into large cubes

Preheat oven to 450 degrees.

Arrange sausage slices in a single layer in a shallow baking dish. Pour in the wine, then sprinkle with parsley and garlic. Bake for 10 minutes.

Serve directly from the dish with bread cubes for soaking up the sauce.

Serves 4-6

TIM'S TIPS FOR PARTY PLANNING

A well-equipped bar is a very important component to entertaining. A few must-have tools, spirits, mixers, condiments and glassware can make a home bar able to satisfy any guest. Start with the basics and build as you go. Always remember to be a responsible host and offer plenty of alcohol-free choices.

COCKTAIL TIPS

Here are a few tips to help you become an expert in developing and making great cocktails.

BALANCE

You want a good ratio of spirit to mixer to create a well-balanced cocktail.

Cocktails go wrong when they are made too sweet. If this happens, add a squeeze of fresh citrus to cut the sweetness.

Try not to overpower the spirit with mixers. Let the spirit shine through as much as possible.

FRESH INGREDIENTS

Always use fresh ingredients and high quality mixers and spirits.

GARNISHES

Keep them cold. Room temperature olives, limes, etc. will raise the temperature of your drink.

GLASSES

Start with cold glassware, directly out of the freezer or chilled with ice and water.

ICE

Big, dense ice is the best to use for cocktails.

Unless a recipe calls for crushed ice, always use large cubes of fresh, solid ice so your cocktail will not become overly diluted.

If a recipe calls for crushed ice, place the large cubes in a clean bar towel, wrap and crush by hitting with a rolling pin or mallet.

Fill ice cube trays with bottled or filtered water to avoid "off" flavors.

MEASURE

Always measure each ingredient.

MUDDLING

Use the flat end of a muddler or wooden spoon to release the oils in a citrus rind, to bruise mint leaves, to crush fruits and more. Don't over-muddle. You just want to release the oils from the items you are muddling, not pulverize them.

SHAKING/STIRRING

Shake vigorously or stir well to chill and dilute your cocktail. This will wake up the flavors and soften the spirit.

Always fill your shaker two-thirds full of ice and shake for a minimum of 30 seconds.

Never shake carbonated beverages.

There is an old myth that shaking or stirring too much bruises the spirit. Nonsense. And, never mind the James Bond myth of shaken versus stirred. Either way is okay as long as you do it well.

When a recipe calls for mixing champagnes with liqueurs such as a Kir Royal (Korbel California Champagne and Chambord liqueur), pour the champagne first, then add your liqueur to help blend as the liqueurs are heavier in density.

FIVE SENSES

Enjoy the cocktail with all of your senses: sight, smell, taste, feel and sound. The feel is how it is balanced and textured when it hits your mouth. The sound; well that is the sound of "Cheers" and the clinking of glasses.

BAR TOOLS AND GLASSWARE

BAR TOOLS

Boston shaker (two pieces: mixing glass and tin)

Cobbler shaker (three pieces: tin, top with strainer and cap)

Good insulated ice bucket that does not sweat when filled with ice

Ice scoop or tongs

Mixing glass

Hawthorn and Julep strainers (the Hawthorn is used when straining from a mixing tin; the Julep is used when straining from a mixing glass)

Sharp knife to cut fruit

Microplane for zesting fruit and shaving chocolate and nutmeg

Juicer (reamer and squeezer)

Channel knife for making twists

Muddler

Wine key or opener

Jiggers (one with 1- and 2-ounce measures, one with ¾- and 1½-ounce measures)

Cutting board

Long-handled stir spoon

GLASSWARE

Three types of glassware will satisfy most cocktails. Look for glassware that is simple in shape and easy to handle, with a thin lip or rim.

Rocks or bucket

Collins or tall

Martini or cocktail

CHECKLISTS

SPIRITS

Bourbon
Gin
Raspberry liqueur
Rum
Tequila
Triple sec or orange liqueur
Vodka
Whiskey

MIXERS

Fresh lemon juice
Fresh lime juice
Lemon-lime soda
Lemonade
Ginger beer
Cola
Club soda
Tonic water
Cranberry juice
Orange juice
Pineapple juice

FUNDAMENTAL CONDIMENTS

Bitters (regular and orange)
Grenadine syrup
Superfine sugar
Cream (heavy and light)
Simple Syrups (page 202-203)
Fresh Sour Mix (page 202)

GARNISHES

Cocktail olives
Cocktail onions
Limes
Lemons
Cherries
Fresh mint
Strawberries
Pineapple
Berries

QUANTITY ESTIMATES

APPETIZERS

Plan to serve 4-6 bites per person, per hour.

The longer your party and the larger your guest list, the greater the number of selections you should offer.

ICE

Plan to use 1½ pounds of ice per person. This will accommodate cocktails and ice baths for beer and wine.

SPIRITS

On average, your guests will have two drinks the first hour, then one drink per hour thereafter.

Note: A 1-liter bottle of spirits will make approximately 22 drinks.

BEER AND WINE BAR FOR A PARTY OF 10

White wine: 3 750-ml bottles
Red wine: 3 750-ml bottles
Beer: 12 bottles or cans light and 12 bottles or cans regular

Be sure to buy accordingly, based on your knowledge of your guests.

Note: A 750-ml bottle of wine equates to an average of 6 glasses.

BAR RECIPES

SOUR AND SYRUP RECIPES

Be sure to let the syrups cool completely before using them and store them in the refrigerator. These syrups are delicious in a variety of drinks, including iced tea.

SIMPLE SYRUP

1 part sugar
1 part water

In a small saucepan, over medium heat, combine the sugar and water. Simmer for 5 minutes, stirring occasionally, until the sugar has dissolved.

MINT SIMPLE SYRUP

1 part sugar
1 part water
1 part packed fresh mint leaves

In a small saucepan, over medium heat, combine the sugar and water. Simmer for 5 minutes, stirring occasionally, until the sugar has dissolved. Remove the pan from the heat, add the mint leaves, stir and let the mixture steep for 20 minutes. Strain before using, pressing on the mint leaves to extract as much syrup as possible.

AGAVE SYRUP

1 part agave nectar
1 part water

In a small saucepan, over medium heat, combine the agave nectar and water. Simmer for 5 minutes, stirring occasionally, until well combined.

HONEY SYRUP

1 part honey
1 part water

In a small saucepan, over medium heat, combine the honey and water. Simmer for 5 minutes, stirring occasionally, until well combined.

SOUR MIX

1 part sugar
3 parts water
1 part fresh lemon juice
1 part fresh lime juice

In a small saucepan, over medium heat, combine the sugar and water. Simmer for 5 minutes, stirring occasionally until the sugar has dissolved. Let cool, then stir in the lemon juice and lime juice.

INDEX

Cheers! :)